D1696182

DUCKIE LEARNS
AN IMPORTANT LESSON

Book 2 of the "Who is Jesus?" series

Written by Stephanie Marie Bullock
Illustrated by Brandon Undeberg

Identifiers:
LCCN:
ISBN: (paperback) 978-1-954926-00-4
ISBN: (hardback) 978-1-954926-01-1
ISBN: (ebook) 978-1-954926-02-8

Available in paperback, hardback, e-book, and audiobook.

Dedication

To all the Parents: Bless you! You are making the most important investment in your child's life. You are taking the steps necessary to teach your kiddo about the most important relationship they will ever have...one with Jesus. So many blessings for you and your family as you walk this journey.

To all the Teachers: I am so impressed by teachers who constantly strive to find new, creative, and inviting ways to share about Jesus. Whether you teach on Sundays or weekdays, you are investing in the spiritual future of each student that God gives you. Thank you for your service!

To all the Influencers: This is for all the grandparents, aunts, uncles, siblings, friends, and others who pour their time, skills, and talents into the children in your life. Thank you, thank you, thank you. You may never know the extent of your influence, but God has placed you in their lives for a purpose. Keep on serving!

To the very talented illustrator: Thank you Brandon Undeberg for the dedication, talent, and time you gave to this project. The adventure has come alive with your work!

To my favorite person: Josiah, you are the best man I know. Thank you for supporting my dreams and ministry as I seek to follow after Jesus. You are a rock star! Thank you for your wisdom, humor, and strength throughout this entire journey. I love you.

~ The beauty around you and the music in you showcase the love of God. ~

Farmer Luke looked over the cow. "Duckie, no!" Duckie looked up surprised. Farmer Luke rushed over and pulled his little friend out of the pond.

Duckie quacked in protest and squirmed to be let go. "What's wrong?"
Farmer Luke tucked him under his arm. "Remember when I told you not to go back into this pond for the rest of the summer? Why were you swimming here again?"
He pouted. "Because I wanted to."

Farmer Luke carried Duckie back to the barn before letting him down. "Duckie, it's very important that you listen and obey me when I say no to something you want to do or somewhere you want to go. You can swim in the horse trough instead."

Duckie did not like that choice. "But it's too small. I want to swim in the big pond!"

Farmer Luke sighed. "I'm sorry, Duckie, but you need to obey me."

Duckie watched until Farmer Luke was out of sight, and then he started to sneak back to the pond. He jumped when he heard a voice call out to him.

"Hey, Duckie! Where are you going?" He turned around and sighed in relief. It was just his good friend Pearl, the dog, and she had her new toy.

Duckie smiled. "I'm going to swim in the pond."
"But I thought we couldn't go there for the rest of the
summer," Pearl said with an eyebrow raised.

"I know that's what Farmer Luke said, but I'm going to do what I want," Duckie said with his wings on his hips.
 Pearl cocked her head to the side. Duckie waited for her to boss him around.
Instead, Pearl asked, "Duckie, do you have time for a quick story? I want to share one with you."
Duckie got excited! Pearl's stories were always very funny.

Pearl smiled and began. "A long, long time ago, in a place called Jerusalem, the people of that great city held a feast once a year."

"A what?"

"A feast. A feast is a big celebration. There are all kinds of amazing food choices; adults love to talk, and children love to play and eat! It's a great time! Anyway, the people of this city were having a feast called Passover. It was a day to remember when God had saved their people from a very bad person through all kinds of miracles."

Duckie held up a wing. "What are miracles?"

Pearl's tail wagged. "A miracle is how God shows us He can do anything." She paused and leaned in close. "Like feeding a whole big crowd with just a little fish and bread!" Duckie's eyes grew big, thinking about how the small hay for one horse could feed a really big herd if God did a miracle. Pearl went on. "Anyway, when Jesus was a young boy, He and His family went to enjoy the feast of Passover with all their friends and family.

When it was time to leave and return to their hometown, the big group of people gathered all their belongings and started back home. They walked a whole day back towards their home. Because this group was so big, Jesus' parents thought that Jesus was somewhere in the group. But He wasn't! Somehow, Jesus was missing!" Pearl said with her eyes wide.

"Wait," said Duckie. "I thought Jesus was their child. Why would He be missing?"

"Well," Pearl said, "I don't know. The important part is not why this happened, but that it did happen."

"When they could not find Him, His parents were so worried about Jesus' safety. They instantly went back to Jerusalem to find him. After three days, they found Jesus in the temple, sitting with the religious teachers and asking them questions. Can you imagine how they felt?

Think about it, Duckie. At this point, Jesus is only twelve years old. He was missing the first day His parents walked back home, the second day they walked back to Jerusalem, and it took three more days once they got there."

Duckie put his wings to his mouth. "Wow, that must have been scary!"

"I'm sure it was," Pearl nodded her head.

"What happened when they found him? His parents must have been really mad!"

"I think they were really worried," Pearl said. "It says in the Bible that Mary asked Jesus, Son, why have you treated us so? Behold, your father and I have been searching for you in great distress. And he said to them, Why were you looking for me? Did you not know that I must be in my Father's house? And they did not understand the saying that he spoke to them. And he went down with them and came to Nazareth and was submissive to them. And his mother treasured up all these things in her heart. And Jesus increased in wisdom and in stature and in favor with God and man. (ESV)"

"Whoa, did Jesus really get in trouble?" asked Duckie. Pearl paused. "Well, we already know from the Bible that Jesus was perfect and never made mistakes, but Duckie, think of this. Jesus is a king, right?"

"Right!" Duckie smiled. He remembered this from his Christmas adventures.

"A king can do whatever he wants!" laughed Duckie.
"Yes," said Pearl. "A king can do whatever he wants. When Jesus had the choice to do whatever He wanted, He obeyed His parents and was submissive to them."

"What does that mean?" asked Duckie.
"It means that Jesus obeyed His parents and trusted their decisions for Him," Pearl said. Then she laid down in the soft grass and let Duckie think about it.

Duckie laid down next to her and looked up at the clouds for a long time.
Finally, he said, "Maybe if a king like Jesus can obey His parents, then I can obey Farmer Luke."
Pearl smiled. "I think that is a good idea."

Duckie waddled over to the big red barn where Farmer Luke
was feeding the cows some hay.
"Hi Duckie!" Farmer Luke said with a smile.
Duckie felt encouraged and so he hopped up on the fence
post and took a deep breath.

"Um, I was going back to the pond today, because I really wanted to go swimming, but Pearl stopped me and told me how Jesus obeyed His parents. Even though He is a king, He still was kind and submissive to them."

Duckie paused and looked down. "So, I wanted to come and say I'm sorry for wanting to do things my way. I will be submissive to you and obey you when you say not to go to the pond for the rest of the summer."

"Oh Duckie," Farmer Luke said with a gentle smile. "I'm not trying to take away your fun. I want to keep you safe."

Duckie furrowed his eyebrows. "Safe from the pond?"

"No, safe from the big snake that now lives in the pond."

"Snake?!" quacked Duckie.

Farmer Luke nodded. "Yes, snake. But even if there wasn't a snake there, I want you to know that I only tell you things to do or not do to keep you safe because I love you."

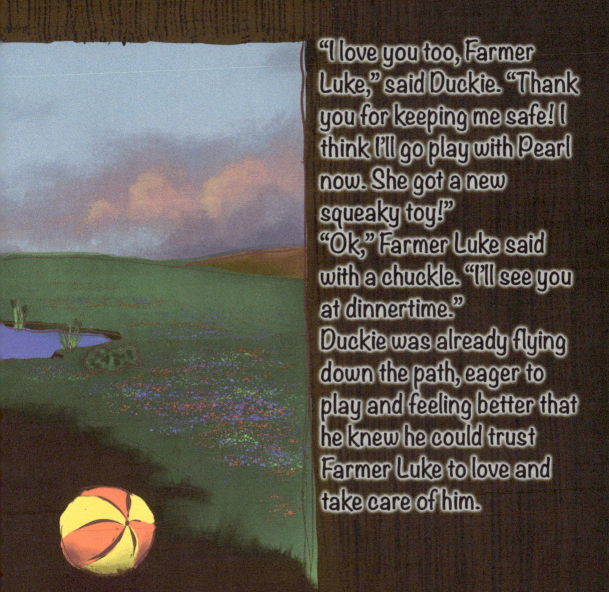

"I love you too, Farmer Luke," said Duckie. "Thank you for keeping me safe! I think I'll go play with Pearl now. She got a new squeaky toy!"

"Ok," Farmer Luke said with a chuckle. "I'll see you at dinnertime."

Duckie was already flying down the path, eager to play and feeling better that he knew he could trust Farmer Luke to love and take care of him.

Note to Parents:
Thank you for reading about Duckie's adventures on the farm! I wanted to offer a few discussion questions in order to help your kids think more about the story's characters. These questions are meant to be a starting point for on-going discussions and are not exhaustive or meant to be asked all at once. Please keep an eye out for more Duckie adventures coming soon as he continues to learn more about Jesus!

Questions:

1. What does Duckie want to do in the pond? Have you ever been to a pond?

2. Can you explain why Mary was so worried about Jesus?

3. What would you do if you were lost?

4. Why do you think Jesus obeyed Mary and Joseph, even though He is king?

5. What would your perfect summer day look like? What would you want to do? Where would you want to go? Who would be with you?

6. Why did Duckie choose to tell Farmer Luke that he wanted to disobey at first, and that he was sorry?

7. Pretend you are a parent. What would you do if you found your kid after searching for a really long time? What would you say?

8. We are going to practice our expressions. Show me on your face how:
    a. Duckie felt when he was told he couldn't swim in the pond.
    b. How Mary felt when she realized Jesus wasn't with the big group.
    c. How Jesus felt when His parents found Him at the temple.
    d. How Farmer Luke felt when Duckie confessed and apologized.

9. How would you feel if you were Pearl and just trying to help a friend obey the rules? How do you help your friends obey the rules?

10. Do people still celebrate Passover? When?

About the Author

Stephanie Bullock is passionate about teaching people who Jesus is. With her background as an educator for nearly a decade, she loves to teach children and introduce them to the person of Jesus Christ. Stephanie struggled with depression and anxiety as a child and remembers the impact Jesus had, and still has, as a source of freedom and joy. Her motto is, "Jesus loves me, this I know!" She and her husband Josiah live in Wyoming.

Contact Stephanie at Stephanie@FreedomSetters.com
to speak at your school or event and visit www.StephanieMBullock.com
for more information on upcoming books, products, and services.

DUCKIE GOES FISHING

Duckie is ready for another adventure. This time, he's going with Farmer Luke to the big ocean! Get ready to learn more about Jesus and fishing in Duckie's new adventure: Duckie Goes Fishing.

CPSIA information can be obtained
at www.ICGtesting.com
Printed in the USA
BVHW060046270822
645597BV00007B/622